# I.

## INFINITE LIFE AND POWER

Man possesses, did he but know it, illimitable Power.* This Power is of the Spirit, therefore, it is unconquerable. It is not the power of the ordinary life, or finite will, or human mind. It transcends these, because, being spiritual, it is of a higher order than either physical or even mental. This Power lies dormant, and is hidden within man until he is sufficiently evolved and unfolded to be entrusted with its use.

*The powers of the sub-conscious mind are dealt with in other chapters. The Powers of the Spirit are far greater and finer than those of the sub-conscious mind.

Thought is a spiritual power of tremendous potency, but this is not the power of which we speak. By thought, man can either raise himself up and connect himself with the "Power House" of the Universe, or cut himself off entirely from the Divine Inflow. His thought is his greatest weapon, because, by it he can either draw on the Infinite or sever himself (in consciousness, but not in reality) from his Divine Source.

Through the Divine Spark within him, which is really his real Self, man is connected with the Infinite. Divine Life and Power are his, if he realizes that they are his. So long as he is ignorant of his oneness with the Divine Source of all life, he is incapable of appropriating the power that is really his. If, however, he enters into this inner knowledge, he finds himself the possessor of infinite power and unlimited resources.

This Power, then, is God's, yet it is also man's, but it is not revealed to him until he is fit to be entrusted with it. It is only when man realizes his oneness with his Divine Source that he becomes filled with Its power. Many teachers and initiates lament the fact that certain secrets are being spread broadcast to-day; secrets that, in the past, were kept closely guarded. They fear that unillumined and unevolved people may make destructive use of spiritual power. This, to the writer, appears to be improbable. It is true that strong personalities, who have a great belief in their own power to achieve and succeed, draw unconsciously on hidden powers, and thus are able to raise themselves high above their fellows. The use, however, that they can make of spiritual power for base purposes is limited, and i not to be feared. There are others, of course, who are misusing their powers. These are black magicians, and while they may do a certain amount of harm, they become reduced, ultimately, to beggary and impotence. There are also others who spend the whole of their spare time searching for knowledge of this very subject. They read every occult book they can lay hands on, but they never find that for which they seek. There are spiritual powers and influences that withhold the eyes of the seekers from seeing, until they are ready for the revelation.

When man, in his search for Truth, has given up all selfish striving after unworthy things, and has ceased to use his self-will in conflict with the greater Will of the Whole, he is ready for the revelation of his oneness with the Infinite. Yielding implicitly to the Will of the Whole may seem, to the unillumined, an act of weakness, yet it is the entrance to a life of almost boundless power.

Man is not separate from his Divine Source and never has been. He is, in reality, one with the Infinite. The separation which he feels and experiences is mental, and is due to his blindness and unbelief. Man can never be separated from Spirit, for he himself is Spirit. He is an integral part of one complete whole. He lives and moves and has his being in God (Universal, Omnipresent Spirit), and God (Spirit) dwells in him. The majority of people are unaware of this intimate relationship with the Divine, and, because they are unaware, or because they refuse to believe it, they are, in one sense, separated from the inner life of God. Yet this separation is only in their thoughts and beliefs, and not in reality. Man is not separated and never can be, yet so long as he believes that he is separate and alone, he will be as weak and helpless as though he actually were. As soon as man realizes the truth of his relationship to the Infinite, he passes from weakness to power, from death unto life. One moment he is in the desert, afar off, weak, separate, and alone; the next, he realizes that he is nothing less than a son of God, with all a son's privileges and powers. He realizes, in a flash, that he is one with his Divine Source, and that he can never be separated. He awakens also to the fact that all the Power of the Infinite is his to draw upon; that he can never really fail, that he is marching on to victory.

It will thus be seen how great is the power of man's thought. While thought is not the power of the Spirit, it is the power by which man either connects himself up with the Infinite Power, opening himself to the Divine Inflow, or cuts himself off and separates himself from his Spiritual Source. Thus, in a sense, man is what he thinks he is. If he thinks he is separate from God and cut off from His Power, then it is as though this were really the case, and he is just as impotent and miserable as though he actually existed apart from God. On the other hand, if he thinks and believes that he is one with the Infinite, he finds that it is gloriously true, and that he is really a son of God. If he believes and thinks that he is a mere material being, then he lives the limited life of a material being, and is never able to rise above it. But if, on the contrary, he thinks and believes that he is a spiritual being, then he finds that he possesses all the powers of a spiritual being.

Again, if he thinks that his work is difficult and that he is not equal to his tasks, he finds that really his tasks are difficult and beyond his powers. Yet on the other hand, if he believes his work is easy, or, at any rate, within his powers, he finds that such is the case, and that he can do his work with ease.

The power within is infinite, for, by faith in it, man is directly "coupled up" with the Spiritual Power of the Universe. The Divine

Spark within him connects him to the Sacred Flame, thus making him potentially a god in the making.

A change then, must take place within man before he can enter into his Divine inheritance. He must learn to think after the Spirit, i.e., as a spiritual being, instead of after the flesh, i.e., as a material creature. Like the prodigal son he must "come to himself," and leave the husks and the swine in the far country, returning to his Father's house, where there is bread (of life) enough and to spare.

# II.

## THE OVERCOMING OF LIFE'S DIFFICULTIES

The true object of life is that man may attain wisdom through experience. This cannot be accomplished by giving in to the difficulties of life, but only by overcoming them. The promises of God are not made to those who fail in life's battle, but to those who overcome. Neither are there any promises that man shall have an easy time and be happy ever afterwards. Yet, it is after this that the majority of people are for ever seeking—an easy life, a good time, freedom from suffering and care. But, in spite of all their seeking, they can never find that which they desire. There is always a fly in the ointment of their pleasure, something that robs them of true happiness; or, possibly, combinations of circumstances conspire to upset all their plans.

Life is a paradox; the true object of life is not the attainment of happiness, yet if we attain the true object of life we find happiness. Those who are ignorant of life's true purpose and who seek happiness high and low, year after year, fail to find it. Like a will-o'-the-wisp, it for ever eludes them. On the other hand, those who recognize the true object of life, and follow it, attain happiness without seeking for it.

In times past, people have made God a convenience. They have thought they could drift through life, learning none of its discipline and then, when in trouble, or things were not to their liking, they could pray to God and have the unpleasant circumstances taken away. The same idea is prevalent to-day. People have left the old orthodoxy and look to various "cults" and "isms" to get them out of their difficulties. They do not believe now that they can curry special favour with God by prayer, but they firmly believe that they can get what they want from the Invisible by demanding it. They think that by this means they can have their own way after all. By this they mean having a good time, with no unpleasant experiences, trials, difficulties, adversities. They are, however, merely chasing rainbows. The easy life they seek constantly eludes them, simply because there is no such thing. The only life that is easy is the life of the strong soul who has overcome. His life is not easy in reality, but appears relatively so because of his strength.

It is impossible to have an easy life, and, if it were possible, then life would be not worth living, for the sole object of life is the building of character and the attainment of wisdom through experience. Life to all of us must always be full of difficulty, and it is to help those, who, hitherto, have found life rather too much for them that this book is being written. What the majority are seeking for is an easy life (which they will never find, but precisely the reverse) and for them I have no message. But to those wise and awakened souls who are seeking for Truth, no matter from whence it may come, and who desire to overcome life and its difficulties, instead of weakly giving in to them, this book, it is hoped, will bring a message.

At this stage we cannot go into the subject of why we should meet with disasters and adversity in this life, nor why some people should have, apparently, a smoother life than others. We must therefore be satisfied to know that we have to meet trouble and overcome difficulty, and that it is only by so doing that we can attain wisdom and build up character. The question, then, is not whether we shall meet the trouble and adversity or not, but rather, how we shall meet them. Shall we be victorious or shall we be submerged? Shall we overcome life's difficulties or shall we give in to them?

The majority of people are drifters on the sea of life. They are wafted here and blown there: they are also carried hither and thither by every current. It is only the few who realize that they have the Power of the Infinite within them by which they can rise superior to all their difficulties, overcome their own weaknesses, and, through victorious experience, attain wisdom.

At this point some practical reader may say that attaining wisdom is all very well, but what he wants is practical help. He is perhaps out of work, has sickness in his house and is in debt. Or, he may be well-to-do, and yet in the deepest distress and misery. To all such I would say that they possess the Power by which they can overcome all their difficulties, and, through overcoming, attain wisdom. A man's success depends, more than anything, upon his faith—his faith in the good purpose of life: his faith in the Power of the Infinite within him and his ability to overcome every obstacle in his path.

The extent of the Power that man can bring into his life is the measure of his faith in that Power. If his faith in It is small, then his life will be feeble and lacking in achievement. If his faith in the Power within him is large, then great will be the power manifesting in his life. The Power of the Infinite is illimitable and inexhaustible: all that is required is an unquenchable belief and trust in it. The weakest and most timid can make use of this Power. There is the same Power in the timid and weak as in the brave and strong. The weakness of the former is due to a lack of faith and belief in the Infinite Power within them.

Difficulties and troubles there will be in every life, and sometimes disaster and heartbreak, when the very earth slides from under the feet, yet, by calling upon the Power within, it is possible to rise from the ruins of cherished hopes stronger and "greater" through experience. Happiness and true success depend upon how the troubles and difficulties of life are met. Adversity comes to all, but if it is met in the right manner even failure can be made the stepping-stone to success. Trouble comes to all, but, while it makes some people stronger and better in every way, it submerges others so that they never rise again. The trouble is the same, it is how it is met that makes the difference. Those who meet difficulty and adversity in the feeble strength of their finite minds and false personality are speedily overwhelmed and broken by the storms of life. But those who rely upon, and have faith in the Power within them, can never be overwhelmed, neither can they ever be defeated. The Power, being infinite, is always sufficient, no matter how great the need may be.

One who realizes his own real spiritual identity, knows that he can never die, that he can never be defeated, that he can never really fail. He may lose his body through the change that is called death; but he, the true man, can never die. Neither can he fail, though he be defeated a thousand times—he must rise again.

Only have faith in the Spiritual Power within you and you can know all the joys of overcoming and achievement. All things will become yours. Seek first the Kingdom within you (your spiritual union with the Infinite, and harmony with the Divine Will and Purpose) and all these things shall be added unto you. You will have no need to fear the morrow, for you will know that all provision has already been made. There will be no need to hoard up wealth, for there will be the necessary daily supplies always available. There will be no need to live near a doctor, for God, the Infinite Life, shall be your health. There will be no need for regret or lamentation, for you shall know that all is well. There will be no fear of future happenings, for you shall realize that the Infinite One makes no mistakes.

# III.

## FATE OR FREE-WILL?

Great has been the controversy in the past, over the vexed subject of fate versus free-will. On the one hand, fatalists claim that man is so closely bound to the wheel of fate it is impossible for him to live his life in any different way than that which is mapped out for him. He can bring a quantity of first-class evidence in support of his claim and believes in his theory with all his heart. On the other hand, the advocate of free-will believes just as wholeheartedly that man is not bound at all, being as free as air. He, too, can bring plenty of evidence in support of his theory, which confirms him in his belief. Each one of them thinks that the other is wrong, yet they cannot both be wrong! Let us therefore examine the subject for ourselves, for it is an important one, being intimately connected with the subject which this book discusses.

First of all, let it be said, they are both wrong, in part, and right, in part. Man is bound to the wheel, yet, at the same time, he has free-will. Let us, therefore, explain this seeming paradox.

It is an ancient truth of the inner teaching that man, when he is unevolved and before he is "unfolded," is bound to the wheel of fate very closely. The unevolved man follows his desires, thus creating for himself a future from which he cannot escape. When however, he becomes more evolved and emancipated, he begins to resist following his desires and strives, instead, to follow higher things. This creates for him a better future and thus he becomes free in comparison with his former slave state. Man is a slave to fate as long as he is a slave to the desires of the earth plane. He is, however, free to overcome lower things and thus rise to higher. When he does this he ceases to create a painful future for himself and thus becomes free.

There is, therefore, fate which is self created. It is necessary to acknowledge this before we can proceed further. One who has not had much experience of life or who has not been a close observer, may deny that there is such a thing, but one who has had great changes in his life, against which he has fought and struggled in vain, knows that there is a purpose working behind the events of life, against which even kings and mighty men are powerless. There come times in man's life when he moves heaven and earth, figuratively speaking: prays until he can pray no more: sacrifices, it may be, his money, his health, his prospects, and does everything that is in the power of a human being in a vain attempt to stave off a threatened disaster. But, in spite of all his efforts, in spite of his cries to a pitiless heaven, the relentless march of fate cannot be stayed. It moves forward like a huge juggernaut and crushes his hopes, his dearest idol, his very life itself or all that then makes his life worth living—and leaves him desolate.

"If then," you may ask, "fate is so pitiless and so powerful, what can be done with it and where does free-will enter into the matter?" In reply it must be admitted at once that it is no use fighting fate. The more man fights it, the more completely he gets broken. There are certain main events in each life which must come to pass. These events and changes are inevitable and it is hopeless to fight against them. While these things, which constitute what we call fate, are inevitable and therefore cannot be avoided, it rests with ourselves how we meet these adversities and disasters. If we meet them in the wrong way they break us. If, however, we meet them in the right way we become stronger through discipline and experience, thus becoming better fitted to bear life's responsibilities and to overcome its difficulties and temptations. One who meets the setbacks, griefs, bereavements and disasters of life in the right spirit becomes a strong and rich character. He becomes mellowed through experience, strong, stable, a helpful influence to all who meet him.

When things go smoothly and life is a merry round, no philosophy or religion seems necessary, and "as for an inward power, what of it, we can do very well without it." So say the thoughtless and inexperienced, but there come times in every life, when, not only is a philosophy, and that a very sound one, necessary, but also a power, of which the finite self knows nothing, is needed in order to raise the soul out of the dust and ashes of its despair. It is one thing to try and meet trouble and adversity in the right spirit and quite another thing to have the power to do so. One who thinks that he has no power within him but that all the power is in circumstances, can never rise victorious over his troubles and become a conqueror over life's difficulties; but one who realizes that he possesses a wonderful power that can raise him up, no matter how crushed he may be, can never be a failure in life. No matter what may happen to him he will play the man and act a noble part. He will rise from the ruins of his life and build it anew in greater beauty and splendour.

At this stage it is necessary to point out that there is a difference between "big fate" and the circumstances of life. "Big fate" as it sometimes is called antedates this present life and its cause does not come within the scope of this little book.* Sufficient if we say here that, through the ages, we reap as we sow, therefore our future depends upon how we meet life and its difficulties now. Big fate, then, cannot be successfully fought, simply because it is the working of Omnipotent Law, but our life generally and its circumstances depend upon how we meet "big fate," and how we recover from it. No matter how seemingly unkind "fate" may be, it is possible for us to make our life a beautiful thing. Inspired and energized by the Power within, we can rise from the ashes of our dead hopes to build anew our life in greater beauty and more in harmony with the Divine Ideal.

*In addition to the "fate" or "future" which every thought and action builds, there is, behind all evolution, a gigantic plan. This wonderful plan that embraces all, from the stupendous conception of a limitless universe down to the smallest electron, is being worked out through the ages with absolute precision. Nothing can prevent this plan from being brought into manifestation. It gathers up our past and weaves it into our present life, just in the same way that it is busily gathering up our present life and weaving it into future fate. It works it all into the big plan, somehow, and with infinite skill. The plan is bound to be followed (this, too, is fate) but HOW we follow it, either with willingness and happiness, or opposition or woe, rests with us (this is free will).

Those who have studied the Occult sciences may say "what about planetary influences?" They will point out that, according to the ancient science of astrology, a man's life is determined by the "star" under which he is born. This is true, if he gives in to the influences around his path. At different times in his life man meets with influences that are sometimes "favourable" and at other times, adverse. These influences are, however, only influences after all, and one who will stand firm during periods of adversity and refuse to give in, relying upon the great Power within to carry him through, will find that he can weather all storms of life and come out of his trials greatly strengthened. He cannot prevent these influences from coming around his path of life, but he can rise superior to them. He will meet with failures and set-backs but he will make of these, stepping-stones to success. He will experience griefs and bereavements, but out of these he will build a finer character and rise to higher things. One, however, who gives in to these things, refusing to rise again and reconstruct his life, condemns himself to further suffering, thus making utter shipwreck of his life.

Let the despairing take heart again. Believe in the Power within you and you will rise to heights before undreamed of. With this Power to help you, you can accomplish the apparently impossible.

Our life here is not governed by a capricious Being who blows first hot and then cold or who favours one person and tortures another. The Supreme Being works through laws that are absolutely just and unchanging. Therefore all disaster and trouble in the life is the effect of certain causes. These causes are our own wrong doing in the past, which set in motion forces, against which the power and wit and wisdom of man are powerless.* However, because the fundamental law of the Universe is love, it follows that the working of the law of cause and effect is not vindictive. Its object is our highest good, viz., to bring us into union with the Divine or in tune with the Infinite. Therefore, by rising up to a higher plane and coming more into harmony and union with the Divine, we rob even big fate of something of its power. We cannot oppose it, for by so doing we fight against Omnipotence, but we can forestall it by doing willingly, and of our own accord, that very thing which experience comes to teach us.

*Another cause is that the soul has failed to learn certain lessons, therefore, in this life, many painful experiences are brought to bear, in such a way, as to teach the necessary lessons. The lessons are, however, learnt only if painful or unpleasant experiences are met in the right way. So long as man believes that he is unjustly treated by fate and that he does not "deserve" what life metes out to him, he intensifies his troubles, both now and hereafter, through not learning the lessons that life desires to teach. When, however man realizes and admits that life is just and that the cause of all his troubles is within himself, he, like the prodigal son comes to himself and, soon afterwards, begins his homeward journey. Yet another cause is that the soul is deficient in character. Strength and stability of character can be built up through the soul meeting trouble and difficulty. Again it must be pointed out that they must be met in the right spirit.

It will be seen then, that our future depends entirely upon the way we think and act in this life. Our future lies in our own hands. If we violate the law of love in this life, we create disaster and suffering for the future, which will have to be met, in the form of "big fate" of a painful character, some day. Therefore, by right thinking and right doing now, we not only ameliorate conditions in this life, but we also create a future that will be more harmonious and freer than anything we have experienced hitherto.

It is also necessary to point out that, even in this life, some of its big disasters are the result of thoughts and actions committed during this present existence. A youth or young man may commit a folly that brings, in after life, a terrible retribution. Or he may do another man a grievous wrong and years afterwards someone else does the same wrong to him. It is always an eye for an eye and a tooth for a tooth on this plane of cause and effect, but the Great Way Shower, by His teaching of the power of love, enables us to rise above these lower things and live a life of harmony and peace.

# IV.

## CAUSE AND EFFECT

Man is the cause of the disasters in his life. He reaps through the ages exactly as he sows. Life is perfectly just and rewards every man according to his works. The fate of the present is the reaping of his sowing in, it may be, a distant past. Therefore, the disasters and sufferings of this life, must not be attributed to the interference of a capricious and unreasonable God, for the truth is, they are due to the exact working of a perfectly just law. Fate, once created, is irrevocable. It can neither be fought nor evaded. By fighting against fate, man merely smashes himself to pieces. To do so, is equivalent to running his head against a stone cliff: the harder he charges, the greater the damage to his head—but the cliff is unaffected. Fate, although largely self-created, is really the Divine purpose of life: therefore, to resist it is to fight against God. Fate, again is not punishment, in any vindictive sense, it is the drawing together of certain remedial experiences, through which the soul can learn the lessons it has failed to learn in past ages and thus attain wisdom. The object of fate is the highest good of the individual, although it may entail suffering and painful experiences.

Because the disasters in man's life are due to past wrong doing, it naturally follows that his future depends upon the kind of life that he lives to-day. If, in the past, he has created for himself a sequence of events and experiences, from which it is impossible for him to escape, it is obvious that his future lives depend entirely upon how he lives the present one. It will be seen that if man can learn the lessons of the present life, and live in such a way as to cease creating trouble for the future, he is beginning to climb the Path of Liberation, which is the road all advanced souls have to follow, or, rather, have the privilege of following. By following this path, man ceases to be bound to the wheel of fate.

This little work does not teach reincarnation, but its teaching is based on a belief that man, in reality, is a spiritual being, a Divine Spark from the Sacred Fire. Spirit being immortal has no beginning or end therefore always lives. This present life is one of countless experiences, each one of which helps to build up character. There is no death, but only changes from one vehicle to another. There is no beginning, or end, or time in reality, these are mere limitations of the human mind. It is impossible for man to die: he can only leave his body. He cannot kill himself, try how he will: he can only force himself out of his body. Man must always go on, whether he likes it or not: he proceeds through the ages, reaping exactly as he sows.

We have already seen that man cannot avoid or fight successfully against fate, but that he can become free from the wheel of fate by living a life in harmony with Divine Law.* At this point it is necessary to point out that most of man's troubles are not caused by fate at all, but are due to his fighting against or trying to resist the great plan. If the experiences of life are resisted, or an attempt is made to evade its discipline, troubles and difficulties will repeat, becoming more painful and insistent until their lesson is learnt and the life changed accordingly. Therefore man has it in his power greatly to improve his present life, as well as to create a far better future, simply by living his life today in harmony with Divine Law.

*This is the inner secret of all esoteric teaching. The new birth, or regeneration, means the awakening of the soul to conscious immortality. The old self, that was bound to the wheel of fate and the plane of cause and effect from which it could never free itself, owing to the fact that it was continually binding itself to the wheel afresh, through following selfish desires, dies, and a new self is born. In other words, the consciousness is raised from the plane of sin and death, of sensuality and desire, of restriction and captivity, to the higher plane of Spirit, where man realizes that he is a son of God. He discovers that the Divine Spark within is his true self. He realizes also that he has always lived—in his real Spiritual Self. Beginning and end, like change and decay, belong purely to the material plane and have no place in Reality. They form part of this present three dimensional existence but have no reality. Endless being is the reality. Anything short of this is mere illusion. It is not necessary, therefore, to believe in the theory of reincarnation or that all our experiences must of necessity take place on this plane. Sufficient to know that we can never die, that we cannot escape from ourselves, and that to neglect seeking with all our heart for union once again with our Divine Source, is merely to prolong our sufferings.

Further, it is necessary to point out that all thought and action have an immediate as well as a far reaching effect. It is true that the full effect of life here is not reaped until after our little course on this plane has been run, but great differences are effected in the present life nevertheless. The way a youth makes use of, or throws away his opportunities, either makes or mars, to a very large extent, his adult career. Opportunities, once allowed to pass, can never be recalled. Sins committed and wrongs done to our fellow men have an unpleasant habit of repeating themselves in a reversed way later in life. For instance, a man may get on in life, and, in his selfish climb, may trample on one weaker than himself, ruining him and driving him to despair. Years afterwards, he will probably be treated in exactly the same way by someone stronger and more favourably situated than himself. Therefore, there is an immediate sowing and reaping that finds fruition in this life. By "immediate" is meant, within the compass of this life. The reaping may be delayed ten or twenty years, but in the writer's experience, it not infrequently comes. "Whatsoever a man soweth, that shall he also reap."

Those, therefore, who think that life is not just, and who whine and complain about the way they are treated, are simply increasing their own troubles. Until man realizes that the cause of all his troubles is within himself he can never do anything to remedy matters, because, obviously, the only thing that is required is for him to change within. Man has to become changed within before his life can be altered. His thoughts, his ideals, his attitude towards life must all become transformed. When this change has been effected, he not only begins to repair his present life, but he creates a fairer and nobler life for the future.

Man, then, has to change. His desires and aspirations, instead of being directed towards hate and evil must be transformed to love and good. Instead of wallowing in lust and selfishness he must lift himself to higher and better things. How can this be done? It cannot be accomplished by the finite man at all, but it can be achieved by the Infinite Power within. It is only when man realizes his oneness with the Infinite and believes that Omnipotent Power is at his disposal, that the Spiritual Power within becomes available. So long as man has doubts and fears or disbeliefs, this special power is not available. It is his, but his state of heart and mind prevents him from either realizing the presence of the Power or making use of it. Before the machinery of a workshop can run it must be connected up with the engine room. In the same way, man, before he can live the new life, must become one with the Infinite Life and Power.

Entering this new life of power, does not take away life's experiences, its trials, troubles and adversities, but the change within does prevent the creation of unnecessary troubles and suffering. Also even a so-called unkind fate loses much of its power to wound, for the higher man rises into union with God and Infinite Love, the less power it has in his life. It still operates, but it fails to wound so deeply, for man, seeing with illumined eyes, knows that it is good that has come to bless; and not evil that has come to slay. Painful fate loses its power to hurt when man ceases to resist it and meets it with open arms, seeking to learn the lessons that it has to teach.

## V.

## SUCCESS

What is meant here by success is the achievement of something worth while, that shall make the world better and richer, and add something to the common good. Our sphere in life may be very humble, but if we overcome our own weaknesses, help others along life's pathway, and do our daily work better than we need, our life cannot be other than successful. If, at the end of our life, we can be thankful for it, realizing that we have made the best possible use of it, we have achieved real success.

Success, to the unillumined, may mean the accumulation of wealth and the winning of fame. Yet those who give up their lives to the acquirement of these things are the greatest failures in life. They gain wealth, it is true, but they find that their money can buy only those things that bring no satisfaction: that it cannot purchase for them any of the things which are really worth having. Success of this hollow kind, can be won, but at too great a price. The greatest Teacher of all once said: "For what shall it profit man, if he shall gain the whole world and lose his own soul?" What does it profit a man if he "gets on" at the cost of happiness, health, joy of living, domestic life, and the ability to appreciate Nature's beauties and simple pleasures?

Yet man must be a striver. He must be for ever seeking better things and to express himself more perfectly. One who drifts through life, making no effort to rise to better things, is not worthy of the name of citizen. Man, if he is to be worthy of the name, must be for ever striving, overcoming, rising. Failure in life is always due to weakness of character. It is only strong characters who can resist the buffetings of life and overcome its difficulties. The man who would make his life worthy of respect and who would rise to high achievement and service, will be confronted by difficulty at every turn. This is as it should be, for it weeds out the weaklings and unworthy aspirants, and awards the spoils to those who exhibit faith, courage, steadfastness, patience, perseverance, persistence, cheerfulness, and strength of character, generally.

Success, especially material success, is not, in itself, of much benefit to the one who wins it. It does not satisfy for long, but it is valuable in other ways. For instance, success, based on service, is a benefit to the community. If, it were not for successful people of this type the ordinary man in the rut would have a bad time. Also, the winning of success builds up character. One who would be successful in the battle of life, must be prepared to be tested and tried in every possible way. One who survives them all is built up in character in almost every direction. Even in his success, however, he will be tempted and tried. One who is engaged in the harsh struggle of business, or who takes part in public life, may, if he does not watch himself very carefully, become hard and callous. Of all failures this is probably the worst. One who succeeds in other directions and becomes a "hard man," is, after all, a sorry failure.

Again, people of the successful, striving, climbing type, are tempted far more than those who are afraid to venture and who remain in the valley of mediocrity. This is true, not only of those who seek to climb the steep path of spiritual attainment, but also of those who are successful in mundane affairs. In each case, they have placed in their keeping great powers and influence such as the ordinary man little dreams of. This is a grave responsibility, for if these powers are used for self-aggrandisement the results are disastrous. Thus, those who climb, are beset on all sides by temptations of a very subtle kind, which, if yielded to, will ruin the life and do grave injury to the soul.

Life is a continual battle. To the ordinary person it is generally a fight with circumstances and the ordinary difficulties of life which are very important in his eyes. The more advanced soul is not troubled much by these things—he rises above them—but he is tempted and tried to a much greater degree, and in a far more subtle manner. Those who think that by following a certain "cult" or "ism," they will be able to have an uneventful walk through life are merely deluding themselves. As he learns to overcome the difficulties of life which baffle the ordinary individual, he will be tempted and tried in other and more subtle ways. This is because life is not for mere passing pleasure, but is for the building up of character, through experience. Therefore, one who would succeed must be strong, and wise and patient. Those who aspire to make their lives really worth while: who desire to serve their fellows more perfectly: who want to build up character through experience and overcome all their weaknesses, inherited or otherwise, must look within for power and wisdom.

It must be pointed out, however, that man must not use his spiritual powers for selfish purposes and self-aggrandisement. There is an immutable law, which has been known to the inner teaching all through the ages, that forbids the use of spiritual powers for the creation of wealth or even of daily bread. Jesus was subject to the same spiritual law, and was tempted exactly in the same way as we. The tempter said: "Command this stone that it be made bread." If Christ had turned the stone into bread, He would have failed in His great mission, but He knew the law. There are thousands of people to-day who are trying, not only to turn, by the misuse of their spiritual powers, stones into bread, but also into motor cars, fat bank balances and lands and houses. Such are heading to disaster, for they are working against the combined Spiritual Power of the Universe. The Enemy of Souls offers those who have learned to tap the inexhaustible Power of the Universe, and who have discovered that they are sons of God, wealth, power, pomp, the applause of men—the glittering things that perish—if only they will misuse their God-given power. Like Jesus, they must refuse. They must put service before self, and give instead of grasping.

Thousands are being taught to-day to force their human will upon life and to use occult powers for the acquisition of wealth and power. They are taught to enter the Silence and demand "what they want." "How to get what you want" is the slogan of these modern teachers. Not merit, not service, not giving, but demanding, compelling by human will-power and by the use of occult forces. This is another device of the Enemy of Souls, and it is taking tens of thousands of seekers for Truth out of the Path. This subject is dealt with more fully in a separate chapter.

If, however, man's ambition is to serve and to give, instead of to grasp and to grab: if, also, he seeks success through merit and not through the misuse of his spiritual powers, he can go forward and the Power will go with him and will help him. When once the Power has been aroused, man must cease all purely selfish striving, although, of course, there will still be much selfishness in his motive. He must seek his success through service and through following noble aims: through merit and a fair exchange, instead of trying to wring success from life, no matter who may suffer thereby.

Further, when this Power has been brought into expression it must only be used in love, for if it used otherwise it will destroy the user. Again, the Power must not be used by the finite human will, but an endeavour must be made to find what the Will of the Whole is, and to work in harmony with it.

Behind each life is the Divine Will and Purpose. Each life is perfect as it is imaged in the Universal Mind. The highest success, indeed, the only true success, is to live the life according to the great Cosmic Purpose, or, in other words, as it is imaged in the One Mind.

Do not imagine, however, that it is the Will of the Universal Mind that man should be a failure or lacking in achievement. Far from it, for we have only to contemplate the Universe to see that the Infinite Mind is for ever achieving and that it never fails. Man, too, must succeed, but let him mix wisdom with his ambition, and work for the benefit of the Whole, rather than for any purely selfish purpose.

It is natural for man to "get on" in life, to a moderate extent.* In order to "get on" he must become more efficient, and thus serve life and his fellows better. Therefore, there is no harm in success of this kind. It is natural and laudable also for one in poor and unlovely surroundings to have an ambition to raise himself to better circumstances. It is only right that he should desire to make life brighter and better for his wife and family. So long as he indulges in ambition wisely, and if he seeks success through better service to his fellows, his is a laudable purpose. If, however, he does not curb and control his ambition but allows it to "run away" with him, he will lose all real joy in life, and, at the last, when it is too late, learn, to his sorrow, that his life, through too much "success," has been a failure.

*It must not be deduced from this that the author deprecates large achievement. There must always be the few who have to bear huge responsibilities. The real success of the lives of these great ones depends entirely upon their motive. If they seek merely power, fame and self-aggrandisement, then their life, no matter how it may appear otherwise, can be only a failure. If, however, their motive is service, then their life is truly successful, no matter how it may appear to be otherwise.

The writer's experience has been that it is necessary that we should always be progressing, achieving, overcoming and endeavouring to succeed. One of the greatest laws of the Universe is progress, therefore it is fatal to stand still. We must go forward, we must achieve, we must accomplish things. If we do so, we may find that many things which cost us much effort, and hard work are not worth the having, yet all the time we are learning, through experience, and are being strengthened and prepared for greater things. Through repeated failure to find true satisfaction we arrive finally at true knowledge, wisdom and understanding. We are wise then, if, with the world at our feet, we can be satisfied with a very moderate material success, and turn our attention and aspirations to higher and better things.

In concluding this chapter let it be pointed out that success and achievement will not drop ready made from heaven into your lap. All who succeed are gluttons for work, toiling whilst others play and sleep. All teaching to the contrary is erroneous. To think that success is going to come to you when it is unmerited, simply because you make use of "affirmations" or employ mental "treatments," is folly of the first water. On the other hand, to use the inner forces in an occult way, so as to compel material things or "success," so-called, in any shape or form, to come to you, is black magic. One who stoops to such practices becomes a black magician, earning for himself a terrible retribution. There is only one way to succeed in the affairs of life, and that is by raising oneself to greater usefulness and service. By doing things better than they have been done before, by bearing greater responsibility, you serve humanity better, and therefore merit success. "It is more blessed to give than to receive," said the Master, and this is true even in the practical and material affairs of life.

First, you must give better and more valuable service: in other words, deserve and merit before you expect to see it materialize. You must sow before you can reap: you must become too big for your present position before you are capable of occupying a larger one. You must grow and expand in every possible way, and as you grow so will your success increase. Outward success is only a reflection, so to speak, of what you really are, and a result of greater and more valuable service to humanity. It requires great effort and determination to get out of the rut, but so long as your ambition is not ignoble or selfish, there will be found within you power sufficient for all your needs.

To win success, either in the hurly-burly of life, or the more difficult path of spiritual progress, demands imagination, vision, courage, faith, determination, persistence, perseverance, hope, cheerfulness and other qualities. These are all to be found within. All these qualities lie more or less dormant within, and can be called into expression if we believe that Infinite Power is ours.

Again, however, must the warning be repeated that this Power must not be used for selfish self-aggrandisement, still less may it be used, or, rather, mis-used, either to influence or dominate others. If this Power is mis-used the results are terrible and disastrous. Therefore, use the Power only for the achievement of good and noble aims and in service which shall enrich the life of your fellows, adding to the common good. Having arrived at this stage you must go forward. There can be no holding back. Ever onward, the Divine Urge is sending you, to greater achievement and accomplishment. Just as surely as the planets must revolve round the sun and fulfil their destiny, so also must you go forward. See to it, then, that your aims and ambitions are based upon eternal wisdom, for upon this does your whole future depend.

# VI.

## HEALTH

It is impossible, in a little work of this description to explain why it is that one person inherits a weak and ailing body and another enjoys a strong and robust constitution. Sufficient for us here to notice that the days of rude, rugged health are passing, and that man is becoming more highly strung, nervous and psychic in his make-up. The old type of rude, unconscious health was due to the animal-like nature of man, which caused his body to be governed more completely by the instinctive mind. Less evolved humans are not affected, apparently, by the mental storms, psychic changes, and spiritual disharmonies that disturb the health of the more evolved types. We have an illustration of this in the case of some forms of insanity. The patient "goes out of his mind," with the result that his bodily health becomes wonderfully good. The instinctive mind takes control of things, and rude, robust animal health is the result. When the patient was sane and his mind filled with worry, ambitions, plans, cares, lusts, hates and griefs, he was probably very far from well. This would be due to the disturbing effects of his thoughts and uncontrolled emotions. When, therefore, his conscious mind gave way and he became happy in an imbecile way, he ceased to think of these disturbing things, with the result that the instinctive, animal mind was able to work undisturbed.

It is of no use sighing for "the good old times," when people were rugged and strong in the way that savages are rugged and strong, for evolution has decreed that man shall change into a higher and more nervous and sensitive type. In this sensitive type wrong thoughts and emotions quickly produce pain and suffering. The majority of people do not know what good health is. Not only do they suffer from minor ailments, such as headaches, indigestion, rheumatism, neuritis, but they also never feel hearty or completely well. They are strangers to the joy of living. Life does not thrill them: nothing quickens their blood: they have no moments of vivid ecstasy—in other words, they do not live, they merely exist at a poor dying rate.

Again, the majority of people are susceptible to infectious diseases and epidemics, yet, if they were really well, they would be immune. Instead, however, of seeking immunity through health, they are seeking it through the use of vaccines and serums, thus adding to the burdens which the body has to bear. All attempts in this direction are bound to end in failure, for, as fast as one disease is suppressed another one will appear.

Many people look upon disease and sickness as inevitable, yet the truth is that health is the normal state and ill-health an abnormality. In tracing back ill-health to its source, we find, first of all, that it is due to disobedience of natural law. Large numbers of people break nearly every known natural law of health, and are surprised that they become ill. Yet the wonder is that they are as well as they are. Yet, while obedience to nature's laws and the use of nature-cure methods will carry us a certain part of the way, we find that there must be causes even deeper than those which are physical. We are confronted by the fact that there are many people who obey every known physical law of health, who bathe, exercise, breathe, eat and drink scientifically, who adopt nature-cure methods instead of drugs and serums, who yet cannot find health. Therefore we must search deeper and go to the mind in order to discover the cause of ill-health.

When we look to the mind we find a prolific cause of sickness. Man thinks himself into ill-health and disease. It is well known that thinking about disease and sickness produces them in the body. People who are for ever thinking about disease, illness, operations and other morbid subjects, become a prey to these things. Those who believe that sickness is inevitable, manifest it in their life. Morbid thinking produces a morbid state of the body, causing it either to fall an easy prey to infection or to break down into chronic ill-health, or even disease. Allowing the thoughts to dwell upon morbid things is a sure way to sickness and invalidism.

Man is not only made ill by his own negative thoughts and emotions, he is also under the hypnotic spell of the race mind. "The God of this world hath blinded the minds of them which believe not." We are all under the spell, more or less, of a huge illusion. The evil, disease, sickness and other imperfections that we see and experience, have no reality, in reality, but have an existence in unreality. Although they are not real in a real sense, yet they are terribly real to this present limited consciousness. By realizing the truth, and by thinking and living in its light and power, the hypnotic spell becomes broken, not completely, else we should not grow old, but to such an extent that a state of greatly improved health can be enjoyed.

We are also hypnotically affected by suggestion, which reaches us from a thousand different sources. The conversations of friends and acquaintances, affect us adversely. Their belief in disease and sickness as realities, and in its inevitableness, colours all their conversation, and, unless we guard against it, this unconsciously affects us. Newspapers, magazines, books, all steeped in the same error, also influence us unless we have become too positive to be affected. From innumerable sources it is subtly suggested to us that disease, sickness, infection are realities that cannot be evaded, and to which we are prone. The effect of all this, putting it in simple and elementary language, is to divert the life power into wrong channels, thus producing disease and ill-health in place of perfection. The normal state of health has to give place to an abnormal state of disease or sickness. The normal health-state is, however, restored when Truth is realized, and the life lived in Its light and power. Absolute Truth and Perfection stand behind all the illusion and imperfection of the sense life. It is by realizing the Truth and the perfection of the Reality, and by establishing the thought-life in Truth, so that our thoughts cease to be negative and based on error and illusion, that health is to be found.

It is often said that ill-health is the result of sin. It is, for thinking about disease, sickness and ill-health, believing them to be inevitable, is one of the greatest of sins. The way of life is to walk (think and act) after the Spirit (which is perfect, whole, immortal and incorruptible) and not after the flesh (corruption, disease, sickness, death). By thinking "after the flesh" we dishonour God who is absolute Wholeness and Perfection, and cut ourselves off from the Divine Life and Power.

But there are other ways by which wrong thinking destroys the health. Thinking thoughts of lust is a prolific cause of unhappiness, sickness and nervous disease. The divine forces of life are directed into a wrong channel, resulting either in indulgence and inevitable weakening of body, brain and will, or in repression and its consequent nervous diseases. If the thoughts are allowed to dwell upon impurity, evil results must follow in some form, either in action or ill-health, or both. Thought must be controlled and reversed continually. Not repressed, but reversed, be it noted, for there is a tremendous difference between the two. Repression creates nervous trouble, but by reversing or transmuting the thoughts the life becomes transformed, and the bodily health greatly improved.

Further, indulging in thoughts of hate, resentment, ill-will, fear, worry, care, grief, and anxiety, produces ill-health, and, by lowering the tone of the body, lays it open to infection and disease. We therefore see that the state of the mind and the character of the thoughts are important factors which cannot be ignored. It is useless to treat either ill-health or disease if they are merely the external effects of hidden causes of the mind. In order to effect a cure we have to get back to the cause of the trouble.

Thought control is a great assistance. Substituting a right or positive thought for a wrong one, will, in course of time, work wonders in the life. In the sub-conscious we have an illimitable power of extraordinary intelligence. According to our thoughts this wonderful power either builds up health, harmony and beauty in our life and body, or just the reverse. The power is good, the intelligence is apparently infinite, but it goes where-ever our thoughts direct it. By our thinking, therefore, we either create or destroy, produce either good or evil. If, therefore, all our thoughts are good, positive and constructive, it follows that both our body and our life must become built up in harmony and perfection. The question is, can this be done? It can be done if we have the desire, and are willing to discipline ourselves and persevere in the face, often, of seeming failure.

Some readers may say, at this point, that they have no desire to be so frightfully good, that they are not prepared to give up lust, impurity, hate, anger, malice and thoughts and emotions of this kind. Very well, if this is so, they must go on and learn, through suffering, the lesson which they refuse to learn willingly.

Others may say: "Yes, I want to control my thoughts, but how can I cease to worry when I have so much about which to worry, and how can I cease to hate when I have been so deeply wronged?" This brings us to an even deeper cause of ill-health than that of mind, viz., the attitude of the heart. Our scriptures tell us that "as a man thinketh in his heart so is he." By "heart" is meant the soul or feeling, desiring part of man. It is here where the conflict between the self-will and the Divine Will, between the desires of the flesh and the longings of the Spirit take place. The real root cause of all unhappiness, disharmony and ill-health is spiritual, and not merely mental or physical. The latter are contributory causes, but the former is the fundamental cause. Spiritual disharmony is, in reality, the cause of all ill-health and disease. Until spiritual harmony is restored, man is a kingdom divided against itself, which, as our Lord said, cannot stand.

Healing, then, must be of a spiritual character. Until this harmony exists there can be no overcoming of hate thoughts, fear thoughts or worry thoughts, and until these are overcome there can be no true healing. Our Lord's healing was a gracious healing of the Spirit. It restored inward harmony by forgiving sin, by changing the heart's desires, by bringing the will of the subject into harmony with the Divine Will of the Whole. Our Lord's healing was not accomplished by means of suggestion, neither was it achieved by human will power; it was done by a bringing into harmony of the heart and desires and will with the Divine Will. At the same time there must have been a revelation of the truth that the Will of God is love, wholeness, joy and perfection, and not disease, sickness and misery.

Mental healing does not become possible until we have made our peace with God. Until we have surrendered entirely to the love principle, we cannot overcome our hate thoughts and malice thoughts or resentment thoughts, by transmuting them into thoughts of love. Until we surrender to the Divine Will and leave all our problems to the Infinite Mind, we cannot cease to worry and fear. Mental discipline and thought-control are necessary after this inward change has taken place, for we all have to work out our own salvation, but the essential thing is the inward heart surrender in love and trust. So long as we hate our brother, or fear what the morrow may bring forth, or worry about the things of this life, we can never be well. When, however, we have become attuned to the Divine Harmony, and have learnt to control our thoughts and emotions and to transmute fleshly and material desires into loving service, a state of wholeness is the inevitable result. Old, deeply-seated disorders die away, and a steady improvement in the state of health takes its place.

In order to regain health it is necessary to raise oneself up continually to the Divine Ideal of health, harmony and perfection. But this is useless if there still remains a clashing of the personal will with the Divine Will, or if there is any hate, malice, envy, or fear in the heart. The will must be surrendered to the greater Will (this, in reality, is our highest good, for the fulfilment of the Divine Will is the happy destiny of man): the heart must forgive and be filled with love; fear must be cast out, and replaced by confidence and complete trust, before we can enter into that happy, carefree, restful state which is necessary for healing. Health is harmony—a delicate balance and adjustment between spirit, soul, mind and body. This harmony is dependent entirely upon the greater harmony between ourselves and God. So long as there is a conflict of will, so long as there is hate or resentment, so long as there is selfishness or while there is fear, this harmony cannot exist. Therefore, the bed-rock cause of health is spiritual harmony, all healing being a restoration of harmony between man and his Divine Source.

When this harmony is restored, man is no longer a kingdom divided against itself, for he becomes established in unity: he works with the Universe and the Divine Laws of his being, instead of against them. The Divine Life and Power flow through him unimpeded, promoting perfect sub-conscious functioning. His thoughts become cleansed at their source ("Create in me a clean heart, O God, and renew a right spirit within me," "Cleanse Thou me from secret faults"). He becomes free from the hypnotic spell of the race mind: his eyes, through the influence of the Divine Spirit, become opened to the Truth; therefore he is no longer blinded by the Prince of this world. In the Divine Union he becomes free. (In Christ all are made alive).

The subject of grief and its effect upon health has purposely been left to the last. No amount of right thinking will prevent bereavements in this life. These form part of the necessary discipline of life, and it depends entirely upon how we meet our trials whether they shall be hurtful or the greatest possible blessing. By rebelling against life's discipline, griefs become hurtful, but the hurt is not in the bereavement itself, but in the attitude of the mind and heart. Until the soul is able to drink the cup of sorrow willingly, and say "Thy Will be done," bereavement is hurtful, destroying both health and happiness. The cause of the hurt is, however, in the hardness of heart, and not in the bereavement itself. There must, therefore, be submission and an acknowledgment that the discipline is necessary. This does not imply, however, a weak giving-in to grief and mourning. One who has been bereaved can never, it is true, be the same again, for he or she becomes more chastened, more loving, more sympathetic, richer and more mellow in character.

The loved one can never be forgotten, but that is no reason why the heart should be bowed down by grief and the life made desolate by sorrow. In such cases true religion, not religiousness, is the only thing that can satisfy the soul, harmonize the mind, and heal the body. To be established in Truth, knowing that all is well: that God makes no mistakes and that there is, in reality, no death but only change, is the only way by which bereavement can be made to be a blessing in disguise. When this stage is reached, grief is overcome, death being swallowed up in victory. The only panacea for all life's troubles is conscious harmony with our Divine Source and the Divine Will and Purpose which desire only our highest good.

# VII.

## THE SECRET OF ABUNDANT SUPPLY

It is a metaphysical truth that the outward life is a reflection of the thought life. Our life is affected by our habit of thinking and attitude of mind, in two ways: first, all our actions are unconsciously influenced by our thoughts, thus helping to bring into manifestation, or attracting to us, an environment that corresponds to our thoughts.* Secondly, we discharge or emit an influence, silent and invisible, that no doubt affects other people. They are probably not aware of it, but they are either repelled or attracted by this silent influence. Thus, if our thoughts and mental attitude are of the wrong type, not only are our actions affected thereby, but also we exert a silent influence that assists in driving the right type of friends, opportunity, success and every possible good away from us. The reverse also is equally true. By right thoughts and a correct mental attitude we naturally attract to us all the good of which our present life is capable.

*This may seem, at first sight, to be a sweeping statement, but two homely illustrations will prove its reasonableness. First we will take the case of a man committed to prison for law-breaking. His environment is obviously due to his wrong actions, the latter being the offspring of his thoughts, for all actions spring from thoughts. Next let us take the case of a man who is the trusted head of an efficient business. Obviously his position is the result of his actions, for he has climbed to it by hard work and faithful service, all due in the first place to constructive thinking and a right attitude of mind.

The Bible tells us that as a man thinketh in his heart so is he. It is equally true to say that as a man is, so does he think, and, that as he thinks, so do his outer life and circumstances become. Therefore, as a man is, so is his environment. This may sound rather metaphysical, but it is really quite simple, and proof meets us at every turn. Take a man from slumdom and put him in nice surroundings, and note what happens. Very soon he either drifts back to a slum or turns his new house into a slum dwelling. Take a man of a higher type, and put him in a slum, and soon he will either leave the slum or change his slum dwelling into a more decent habitation. Put a slut in a mansion, and she will turn it into a pig-sty, but put a woman of a higher type in a hovel and she will make it clean enough to entertain royalty. Therefore, before you can change a person's environment it is necessary to change inwardly the person himself. When a man becomes inwardly changed and filled with new ambitions, ideals and hopes, he, in course of time, rises above his sordid surroundings and attracts to himself an environment that corresponds to his new state of mind. It would be useless to tidy up the house of a slut for her, for she would soon make it like a pig-sty again, but if you could get a new ideal of neatness, cleanliness, order and spotlessness into her mind, she would not rest satisfied until her immediate environment corresponded, in some measure at least, to her mental ideal or image.

Very often, the failures of a man's life, and its disharmonies and poverty, either comparative or real, are outward symbols of his weakness of character. He may have ability in plenty, but he may lack application or steadfastness, and thus he fails in all his undertakings, and has to be kept by his wife and daughters. He will assure you that his circumstances are due to ill-fortune, but the actual cause of his failure is in his character, or, rather, lack of character.

If, therefore, a man's poverty and lack, or financial difficulties are due to weakness of character which manifest in his work and dealings with others, in the form of inefficiency, poor service and bad judgment, it follows that he, himself, must change before his circumstances can be permanently altered for the better. The difficulty in dealing with unsuccessful people is in getting them to realize that they, themselves, are the cause of all their troubles. Until, however, they do realize this, their case is hopeless, and it is impossible to help them, but when they acknowledge that the fault is theirs, they can be shown that there is a remedy for their ills and a way out of their difficulties, by means of self-improvement. Let them then search for hidden weaknesses, and build up those weak places in their character, such as lack of grit, determination, steadfastness, persistence, patience, probity, decision, which are the cause of their troubles, and they will find that their circumstances will gradually change for the better. Everything comes from within—first within, then out, this is the law—therefore the change must always take place within.

Going more deeply into the subject and becoming more metaphysical, it is necessary to point out that the cause of all manifestation is Mind. We have already seen that a man's mind and character are reflected in his circumstances; now let us think, for a moment, about the Mind that is Infinite. The whole universe, which is, of course, infinite in extent, has its origin in the Divine Mind, and is contained within this Infinite Mind, just in the same way that you can hold a mental picture in your own mind. God's Universe, as it is imaged in the Divine Mind, is perfect. We see it as imperfect, because we only receive a finite sense-perception of that which is perfect and infinite, from this forming, in our minds, an image that is necessarily imperfect and finite, which we project outwards, and, not knowing any better, think is real. But the universe, as imaged in the Divine Mind, and as it actually is in reality, is both infinite and perfect: it is also infinitely perfect. There is no poverty or lack in a universe that is infinitely perfect, whole and complete in the Divine Mind. Poverty and lack have their origin in the mind of man: they have no place in the Mind of God.

We cannot, in a little elementary work of this kind, go more deeply into this extremely fascinating subject. Sufficient if we say here that the only Reality is infinite perfection and wholeness, therefore there cannot be any lack at all (in reality). The obvious lack and poverty that we see around us are the product of the human mind. Those who live in a consciousness of poverty and lack, go through life closely fettered by limitation. They can never escape from poverty, it dogs their footsteps like their shadow. In fact, it is a shadow or reflection, in the outer life, of their state of mind and mental attitude.

On the other hand, those who live in a consciousness of sufficiency, are not troubled about supply. Their circumstances reflect their type of mind and mental attitude. It does not follow that they will be rich, for many of them prefer to live from hand to mouth, and quite large numbers of people have no desire whatever to possess wealth of any kind, but they have no worry about supply, for their needs are always met by sufficiency.

Many of our readers look upon the possession of wealth as an iniquity. Personally, I do not see how, at this stage, it can be altogether avoided. Capital is necessary for the conducting of business and for the carrying out of enterprises, but, as far as the hoarding of wealth is concerned, I certainly think that it is both unwise and unnecessary. There is nothing more deadening to the spiritual life than riches. There is always hope for the drunkard and the harlot, but it is most difficult although, of course, not impossible, for one who is burdened by wealth to enter the kingdom of heaven. Some are able to do so, but they are allowed to enter simply because they hold their wealth as of no importance, merely as something of which they are stewards for a season.

The hoarding of wealth is just as unnecessary as poverty. They are both based upon a fundamental error. This error is in thinking that all supply, being material, must necessarily have a material source: that it is limited in quantity, and therefore must be grabbed at and fought over. The truth is, of course, that the source of supply is Spiritual, and therefore without limit; consequently, one who realizes the truth has no thoughts of poverty or lack, and ceases to fear it. On the other hand, he has no incentive to hoard or to grab wealth, for of what use are riches to one whose supply is for ever assured?

All who enter into this truth regarding supply, either despise riches or hold them very lightly indeed. They cease to have any desire for wealth. Why should they have any such desire? People hanker after wealth because they fear poverty with a deadly fear, and long for wealth because they think that its possession would release them from their fears. When, however, they know the truth, they also KNOW that their wants will always be supplied, therefore they no longer desire wealth and its cares and responsibilities.

Wealth is just as abnormal as poverty. Our Lord showed this to be the case by choosing to be poor (but not in poverty) and by His teaching in the Sermon on the Mount. What Jesus promised was adequate supply, but not wealth or riches, to those who had sufficient faith in their "Heavenly Father." any people live this planless life of utter dependence upon their Spiritual Source. They never become rich, but all their needs are supplied. Something always arrives in time to meet their requirements. Such a life requires a very live and active faith, but its results are as certain as the rising of the sun.

An understanding of the truth regarding supply is a necessary foundation for the faith without which the planless life is impossible. It is necessary to _know_ the utter falseness and unreality of poverty and lack before we can trust in Divine Providence or the working of Spiritual (at the same time, mental) law. It is necessary to know that the universe is Spiritual: that God is Spirit, in whom we live and move and have our being, and that because we are a part, very small, but yet a part, of the Whole, all our wants, all through the ages, must be supplied. Supply, sufficient for all our needs, is the reality. Poverty and lack, the product of lack of faith, of fear, of ignorance, of weakness of character, have their origin in the human mind, and are the unreality--the negative which has no permanence or reality.

When we have learnt the truth, it is necessary to live in the Consciousness of it, and to think and act and praise God as though sufficiency were already ours. Not to spend money that we cannot afford to spend, nor to incur debt, but to live mentally in an atmosphere of abundant supply. We have to remember that the change in consciousness must take place first and become well-established, before its effects can be seen to manifest in the outer life.

The entering of this higher consciousness where we know and realize the truth, viz., that the Source of all our supply is Spirit, and that the Divine Source is limitless, is not easy, although it is less difficult to some than to others. It demands constant mental activity and watchfulness: it requires persistence and perseverance in right thinking, yet it is possible to those who are in earnest. By living in the consciousness of God's Supply and exercising a lively faith, the life becomes affected, principally due to both conscious and unconscious change of action.

Having dealt with the esoteric or inner side of the subject of supply, I will now treat it more from the outer or practical side, the latter being, of course, just as important as the former.

The teaching of this chapter does not discourage industry and thrift, far from it. After the Lord Christ had fed the five thousand, all the leavings were carefully collected so that nothing should be wasted. This is in accord with Universal law. There is a law of economy both in the natural and spiritual worlds. Nature appears, on the surface, to be very wasteful and prodigal, but, actually, she never wastes anything, if it can be avoided. Therefore, the action of the disciples was in accord with universal law. What a lesson for us! To be careful and saving is a mark of superiority both in mind and character. The wastefulness of the helpless poor is notorious. Those who are "well to do" are far more careful and conserving than the very poor. There are exceptions, it is true, but the rule is that a man who cannot save money has not it in him to command success in life. Inability to deny himself certain things shows a weakness of character and lack of purpose which make success impossible.

Two men that I knew very well built fortunes upon , which they saved out of meagre earnings. It is always the start that is difficult: if you cannot overcome the preliminary difficulties you have not the steadfast purpose to hold your own in the battle of life. in On the other hand, once the initial difficulties have been overcome, it is not difficult to get your barque into the currents of prosperity. When once you realize that there is unlimited abundance in which you can share: when once you learn to live in the consciousness of this abundance, at the same time living within your present income and doing your present work as well as it is possible for it to be done, you have set out on the path to affluence.

One who realizes and really believes that there is abundance and plenty for him, puts into operation a powerful law which will surely bring opportunity to him, sooner or later. Many, however, ruin their hopes by not knowing that for a time they must live a kind of double life. They must be opulent in consciousness, but careful and thrifty in actual practice. The time will come when their means will largely increase, then, if they are wise, they will live on part of their income, instead of living up to it. This will give them a wide margin for charitable purposes, for the taking up of further opportunities and for extensions. Many business men have to let golden opportunities pass, simply because they have saved little or nothing, owing to lavish private expenditure, or they have to let other people in to share their schemes who, in addition to taking a large share of the profits may prove a serious handicap and hindrance in other ways.

While in its essence, the Source of Supply is spiritual, it comes to us through material channels, and, in order to have a share in it, it is necessary to earn it. We have to give something in exchange for what we draw from life in the way of supply. We must give in order to receive, and what we give must be something that the world wants or needs.

The secret of supply is, then, to realize that there is unlimited abundance and to live in the consciousness of it, as completely as though no material channels existed, and, at the same time, to work as zealously and be as careful as though there were no such thing as spiritual supply. At the same time we must give the world something that it wants, or otherwise serve in some useful capacity, exercising honesty, probity and justice in all our affairs. It is folly to expect abundance to drop ready-made in our lap; it must be earned by intelligent and faithful service.

Being a retired business man who started life with nothing, not even good health, I have looked at this subject from a business man's point of view. The principle applies, however, to every walk in life, and each reader can adapt the teaching of this lesson to his or her particular needs.

# VIII.

## THE POWERS AND LIMITATIONS OF THE SUB-CONSCIOUS MIND

The sub-conscious mind is the mind of Nature. It possesses extraordinary powers and intelligence, but no inspiration. It is instinctive: it is animal: it is natural: but there is nothing god-like about it—it is of the earth and the physical plane. It can be described as the inner forces of Nature resident within our body. Having said this we have said nearly all there is to be said about the sub-conscious, yet this is the mind of which some people have made a veritable god.

The sub-conscious mind, if led aright, is a very good friend, reducing all repeated thoughts and actions into habit, which, in time, become settled and part of the very life itself. Thus, by conscious right thinking and conscious right action, a good habit is formed, which becomes, in course of time, practically automatic. This, of course, builds up the character, which, in turn, affects the life. It will be seen then, how important is the right use of this willing and faithful servant. It is no god, it has no inspiration, but it is a very useful servant, as we shall see.

Most of our actions or movements are done or made sub-consciously. The reason that "practice makes perfect" is that the sub-conscious mind learns to do the task, and, by so doing, takes it off our hands. How difficult it is to learn to drive a motor-car. How carefully, at first, we have to double de-clutch and obtain the right engine speed for a noiseless "change," yet, after a time, the whole action is performed sub-consciously. It is the same with pianoforte playing. Many players, some better than others, can play the most difficult classical music without consciously recalling it to mind. As soon as they try to remember the whole "piece" leaves them, but as long as they leave the whole matter to the sub-conscious (which never forgets) they can keep on playing. I and my conscious mind are not doing much of the actual writing of this book. We think the thoughts and have something to do with the formation of the sentences, but the sub-conscious mind writes them down. If I had to think of each word and letter, my task would be hopeless, and I should become half dead with fatigue.

The sub-conscious mind, however, is even more helpful, for it does the bulk of our thinking, and can be taught to do a great deal more. If we had to think everything out laboriously, according to the laws of logic, life would be unbearable. Instead of this our sub-conscious mind does the bulk or our thinking, and, if we give it a chance, will do it in an extremely accurate manner, strictly according to the laws of logic and without the slightest fatigue. The more that we train the sub-conscious to do our ordinary thinking for us, the less we suffer from fatigue. Fatigue is unknown to the sub-conscious mind, therefore we can never tire it or overwork it.

The sub-conscious mind can be made to do more and more work for us if we will delegate definite work for it to deal with. One who has learnt thought control, who can take up a matter, consider it in all its bearings, and then dismiss the subject from his conscious thought, is able to increase his efficiency a hundred per cent., and reduce his mental fatigue almost to vanishing point. Instead of laboriously working out his problems and worrying and scheming over them, he simply dismisses them to his sub-conscious mind to be dealt with by a master mind which works unceasingly, with great rapidity, extreme accuracy and entirely without effort.

It is necessary, however, to give the sub-conscious every available information, for it possesses no inspiration or super-human wisdom, but works out logically, according to the facts supplied to it.

This great, natural, untiring "mind downstairs," as it has been called, is also capable of doing even more useful work still. A writer or speaker, or preacher can collect notes and ideas for his article, book, speech or sermon, and pass them down to his sub-conscious mind with orders that they be arranged in suitable order, division, sub-division and so on. When he comes either to write or prepare the notes of his speech or sermon, he will find all the work done for him, and all that he has to do is to write it down, entirely without effort or fatigue.

Again, a business man who has learnt to make use of his sub-conscious mind in this way, need not juggle or worry or fatigue himself by planning and scheming for the future. All that he need do is to submit the facts to the "greater mind downstairs," and all the planning will be done for him, entirely without effort, and far more efficiently than he would have done it through laborious conscious thinking.

The following, which has just been brought to my notice, is a striking confirmation of the teaching of this chapter:-

In a recent issue of Collier's Magazine, an interview with Henry Ford appeared. He spoke of the way with which big business men deal with problems, and pointed out that they did not spend a lot of time pondering and puzzling over plans or ideas. He said: "An idea comes to us: we think of it for a little while, and then we put it in the pot to boil. We let it simmer for a time, and then take it out." What Henry Ford means, of course, is precisely what we have been saying, viz., that the idea or problem is dismissed to the sub-conscious mind, which works it out, and presents it to the conscious mind for judgment.

Yet again, an inventor or one who is constructing something mechanical, can make use of the sub-conscious mind in precisely the same way. Let him sum up the whole problem, arrange all his facts and available information, and pass them all to his sub-conscious mind, when, if a successful result is within the range of possibility, an answer or idea will be forthcoming. All this being done, mark you, without any effort whatever.

All this may seem, especially to some readers, rather wonderful and far-fetched, yet there is nothing occult or mysterious about it. I am perfectly sure that there is no great writer, politician or business man who does not make use of his sub-conscious mind in this way. He probably does so unconsciously, but his procedure is the same. Some employ the whole of their mind naturally. These become men of achievement, who occupy responsible positions, and who bear immense burdens without strain, worry or care. Responsibility sits lightly upon them, and they are serene and untroubled when in positions, and when confronted by tasks and difficulties, such as would drive an ordinary individual out of his mind. Such men develop their powers of attention and concentration (anyone who is in earnest can do this) to a very high degree. They are at great pains to get to the root of a problem, and obtain all the available data possible, but, after that, it is their sub-conscious mind that does all the work, and which arrives at a decision.

While it comes natural to a few to use their sub-conscious mind in the correct way, the majority of people find themselves unable to do so. Such, however, can acquire the art by training. First, it is necessary to learn thought-control, so as to be able to take up a problem or dismiss it entirely from the mind at will. When a problem is passed on to the sub-conscious to be worked out, the subject must be dismissed entirely from the conscious mind. The problem must not be worried over, nor the thoughts allowed to dwell upon it; it must be left entirely to the sub-conscious. Second, every possible detail and information connected with the problem must be grasped by the conscious mind, and the whole matter, pro and con, visualized before being passed to the sub-conscious. It will be seen, then, that thought-control of a high order is necessary, also powers of attention and concentration. These can all be developed by anyone who is really in earnest.

A good way of starting the use of the sub-conscious mind is to hold the problem in the mind just as one is going to sleep. There must not, upon any account, be any attempt made to solve the problem or to worry over it. Instead, the main facts of the case, on both sides, must be marshalled, and the case presented to the sub-conscious mind in much the same way as you would place it before your lawyer. Having done this, dismiss the whole matter to your sub-conscious mind, and in most cases you will find in the morning that a solution has been arrived at without any effort or fatigue on your part.

This, of course, is only one of the many ways in which the sub-conscious mind can, and does, serve its master, or the one who should be master. This great invisible force of Nature is for ever working. Whatever ideal is held in the mind becomes woven into the life through the tireless working of the sub-conscious mind. Only set your attention upon high and lofty achievement, and you will focus all the invisible inward forces of Nature upon its accomplishment. In course of time you will reap as you sow. If you will direct your attention into the right channel, backing it up with energetic, conscious action, your sub-conscious will help you day and night, thus making success and achievement possible.

# IX.

## THE USE OF THE SPIRITUAL OR SUPER-CONSCIOUS MIND

We have already seen that the sub-conscious mind, wonderful though it be, is instinctive merely, lacking inspiration and what we call originality.

All inspiration comes from the Universal Mind, via the super-conscious. All poets and inspired writers get their inspiration in this way. This higher mind is not recognized by Psychologists, but it has long been known to searchers for spiritual truth.

What we get from the sub-conscious is the outcome of facts and knowledge supplied to it. What we get from the super-conscious is direct inspiration from higher planes. This higher mind might also be called the Mind of Illumination, for those who can enter into it become illumined, being able to know the Truth and to see things as they really are, and not as they falsely appear to the senses.

This limited consciousness in which we live is bounded by our five senses. The universe that we see around us is partly real and partly an illusion. The real universe is Spiritual and infinite: what we sense is a limited, partial conception of a fragment of it. Our limited, finite conception of the universe is entirely misleading and erroneous, and so long as we rely on sense evidence and the human mind, we remain in darkness and uncertainty. When, however, we can rise into the super-conscious realm, our consciousness expands, transcending the senses and the limitations of the physical plane.

The Spiritual mind is, of course, only accessible to those who are more delicately attuned to its finer vibrations. Nothing that is worth having can be had without effort, and it is only after much self-discipline that it becomes possible for the student to raise his consciousness to this higher realm and understand life from the standpoint of the Universal Mind.

There is nothing, either mystical or psychical, about the use of this higher mind. One who makes use of it becomes spiritually-minded, that is all. He does not go into trances, nor need he become clairvoyant: he simply remains a sane, normal individual, with this difference only—he makes use of more of his mind than does the ordinary individual.

One who is able to use this higher mind develops that which has been termed "the divine quality of originality." If ever a person is to rise above the dead level of mediocrity it must be through direct inspiration from higher planes, through his super-conscious mind. If ever a person is to bring forth a new idea which shall enrich humanity and add to the common good, it must come through the higher mind.

One who is properly attuned, becomes, through the super-conscious mind, a recipient of knowledge that is above human, and wisdom that is divine. He knows by direct knowing: he becomes wise through an influx of Divine Wisdom. He is able to distinguish between the real and the sham, between the gold and the dross: he is also able to see and recognize the right path in life—a thing utterly impossible to the mind of the senses—and to tread it, thus being led into the only true success and real good of which his life is capable.

Let it be said here that all Wisdom must come from within. While books and the written word may be helpful, it is the Spirit within the reader that illumines the word, and makes it real and true to the seeker after Wisdom. One who realizes that he is illumined within by the Divine Spirit, and that this alone can bring him into real knowledge is well advanced on the path that leads to realization.

The wisdom of the human mind always leads to disappointment. It is based on the evidence of the senses, which is erroneous, therefore its findings must always be lacking in real wisdom. One who relies upon the inspiration of Divine Wisdom has often to decide to take a course of action which, apparently, is opposed to his best interests. Yet, if he follows the inward Wisdom, he finds that he is always guided aright, and, later, has cause to be devoutly thankful that he followed the gleam.

# X.

## CHARACTER BUILDING AND THE OVERCOMING OF HABIT

Character building is the greatest object in life. It has been said that character is the only thing we can take with us when we depart this life. This is perfectly true, therefore the object of all religion (not religiousness), mental training and development should be the building of character. A religion that does not build up character is worthless. Those who think that they can "flop" through life, avoid, as far as possible, its discipline, make no effort to improve their character, and through believing in a certain creed can miraculously become perfect, simply by dying, are deceiving themselves. We do not become "perfect," i.e., of a strong and perfect character, either by believing in a creed or through dying, but by attainment. God helps those who help themselves, and those people who will not strive after better things cut themselves off from all the glorious and wonderful possibilities of attainment.

Before, however, thinking about such lofty things as entering the Path of Attainment, and becoming changed into, and modelled after the Divine Image, the average person may wish to know how to overcome bad habits and weaknesses of character which are keeping him down in life, and, possibly, undermining his health. Most people are conscious of some wrong habits that ought to be overcome, and weaknesses of character which should be eradicated. Possibly they have fought against their habits or weaknesses for years, prayed until they are tired of praying, made innumerable attempts at turning over a new leaf, yet all in vain, for they are as firmly in the toils as ever. Many people give up the struggle and endeavour to lead a sort of Jekyll and Hyde existence, being outwardly a Christian or righteous person, but inwardly something quite different. Yet they find no satisfaction in this dual life, for they know that they are drifting towards an abyss.

Yet there is a way of escape that is open to all. The Infinite One has provided man with powers that are apparently unlimited: powers which can be used either to build up the life and character or to destroy them. These powers are those of the sub-conscious mind. This mind is a reservoir of unlimited, tireless forces, and becomes, if we use it aright, our best friend, or, if we mis-use it, our worst enemy.

Every time a bad action is indulged in, wonderful changes take place in the nervous system, and energy becomes stored up in certain cells, so as to make it easier to do the wrong act on a future occasion. It is equally true that every time a good action is done, similar changes, but in a reverse direction, take place, that make the doing of the same action easier in the future. This explains the tremendous power of habit. Our body, brain and nervous system become changed, either for the worse or the better, according to the type of action indulged in.

We do not yet fully realize what a wonderful adventure life is. We are entrusted with tremendous powers, and by their use or mis-use we can either destroy ourselves or build up our character in every possible direction. What a responsibility, yet what a glorious opportunity!

In order, however, to find a way of escape from evil habit and weaknesses of character, we must go deeper than actual deeds, for actions are effects of hidden causes. The cause of all action is thought. A thought, someone has said, is an action in the process of being born. It is true that we possess primitive desires and impulses, but these can be transmuted into noble actions and high achievement simply by directing the thoughts and attention to higher and better things. For instance, the powers of sex become transmuted into brain power if the thoughts and attention are completely transferred from sex to intellectual pursuits. If, however, the thoughts are allowed to dwell upon sex or passion, then the kingdom becomes divided against itself, and man begins to drift towards the abyss. The strain of modern life is filling our asylums, yet there are those who can work fifteen or even eighteen hours a day and thrive on it, although engaged in severely-trying brain work. These have learnt to transmute their lower powers into higher. This is not done by means of esoteric or occult practices, but by obeying the Divine Injunction to set our affections on things above. In other words, to keep our thoughts and attention fixed upon higher and better aims, ambitions and pursuits.

It is impossible to overcome bad habits by fighting them, for the more we fight them the stronger they become. The injunction to "resist not evil" is very applicable to habit. The way of escape is not by fighting evil or wrong habit, no matter what its character may be, but by concentrating upon building a good habit that shall cut the ground from under the feet of the bad one, or by turning the attention to higher and better things.

Whatever we fix our attention upon, or whatever it is that we idealize, our sub-conscious mind endeavours to actualize and make real in our life. By fighting a habit we direct sub-conscious attention to it, and this is fatal. If, however, we turn our whole attention to something entirely different and which is higher and better, all the powers of the sub-conscious are directed towards the production, in the life and body, of the new object of attention.

We see, therefore, that we do not have to overcome habit. If we did our task would be hopeless, for the human will is helpless before the power of the sub-conscious mind. The sub-conscious powers can be led by the imagination, but they cannot be coerced by the will. The will must be used not to fight the habit, but in raising and directing the attention to something higher and better. By this means a new habit is formed. The attention of the sub-conscious mind is taken away from the bad habit, and all its powers directed towards the creation of a new and better one. The sub-conscious does not care what the habit is. It is indifferent as to whether it is good or bad. It is just as willing to produce a good habit as a bad one. We, each of us, therefore, hold our fate in our own hands. We can, by controlling our thoughts and imagination and by directing our attention to better things, focus all the powers of the sub-conscious on the building up of good habits, or, on the other hand, we can, by allowing our thoughts and mental pictures to dwell upon undesirable things and our attention to be directed to low or weak ideals, fall into undesirable habits. The power that produces the habits is the same in each case; it is the way in which this power is directed that is the vital and essential thing.

It is very necessary to point out that right thinking and correct use of the imagination must be accompanied by corresponding right action. Many people make use of auto-suggestion and expect it to destroy their bad habits and build up better ones, but it never will, or can do so, unaided. Auto-suggestion is useless if it is not followed by constructive action. Young people should expend their energies in physical culture and games. Older people should interest themselves in hobbies and intellectual pursuits. It is only advanced students who can control their thoughts so that they can govern their life forces by mental means. Those less advanced, when attacked by evil or weak thoughts, must get up and do something quite different, and thus get their minds off the forbidden subject and interested in the new object of attention. It is a case of directing the desires and life forces into different channels, by controlling the thoughts and attention. Here is seen the value of true religion, for it brings fresh ideals into the life and directs the attention to higher and better things. The writer realizes that a change must take place in the heart of the individual before he can desire these better things. When, however, this change has taken place, the battle has only just begun, for each one has to work out his own salvation.

At first, then, most people will find it necessary to do something in order to attract their attention and guide their thoughts to something quite different from the forbidden subject. Later on, however, when they become more advanced in the science of right thinking, they will be able to direct their thoughts into any desired direction. This necessitates constant vigilance. Each thought has to be carefully scrutinized before being allowed to pass the threshold of the mind. By reversing every negative or unworthy or ignoble thought into its opposite, a change is wrought in the brain and nervous system. The cells formerly used for wrong thinking and for the production of wrong action go out of use as new cells are brought into use for the production of right action.

This stage leads to one higher still, when it becomes a settled habit to reverse bad thoughts into good ones and perform right actions instead of bad or weak ones. The power of the sub-conscious mind, which at one time seemed so evil, produces right action more or less automatically. When once the habit of cleaning the teeth is established there is experienced an uncomfortable feeling until they have been attended to. When once a dirty person has learnt to wash himself thoroughly and keep himself decent, he will feel uncomfortable if he gets dirty. The same rule applies in the more important things and habits of life. If those who are in the bondage of habit will only direct their thoughts and attention to the building up of good habits, their old weaknesses will die a natural death.

It must not be thought that the victory over life-long habits is easy. It may seem so at first, but sooner or later temptation will come with added force, which may result in a sad fall. If this should happen it is most important that too much attention should not be paid to the incident. Instead, the beginner should pick himself up, and, making a mental note of the immediate cause of his downfall, thus benefiting by the experience, press on again towards freedom. It is most helpful to realize that not only is the sub-conscious mind willing to be guided aright, if we will only persevere long enough (until persevering itself becomes a habit), but that we also have behind us all the Spiritual powers of God. The Infinite One sees to it that the odds are not overwhelmingly against us.

Our difficulties are not insuperable, although they may appear to be so. We can always win through if we faint not. Heaven looks on with sympathetic interest and rejoices with the struggler when he succeeds, and mourns with him when he fails. The struggle is a stiff one, for it is only by this that the seeker after God can become strong in character, but the victory can always be won. When the situation appears hopeless, let the struggling one remember that there is a way of escape somewhere, and that God, who is his freedom and deliverer, will reveal it to him if he faints not. If all who seek deliverance will realize that the Power of the Infinite is on their side, and that they are bound to become victors if they will only keep on, they must succeed. And what a joy is theirs! There is no happiness quite like that which comes to one who has fought the good fight and overcome habit and weaknesses of character.

May every reader experience this supreme joy of overcoming.

# XI.

## HAPPINESS AND JOY

Deep down in every heart is an unquenchable desire for happiness. The advanced soul desires happiness just as much as the pleasure-seeking worldling, the difference between them is simply that the former, through knowledge and experience, does not search for happiness, knowing that it can never be found by direct seeking, but finds it through service and love to others and in victory over self; while the latter seeks happiness, like a will-o'-the-wisp, in every form of pleasure, and finds it not.

Man is never satisfied with his life: he is for ever seeking something that is better. Until he learns wisdom, he looks for it in pleasure, in sense gratification of various kinds, in wealth, luxury and possession. The less evolved a man is the more convinced he is that happiness can be gained in these ways, and the lower are his desires. For instance, those who form what is called the underworld of our cities, seek happiness in vice and debauchery. Those who are more evolved seek pleasure in more refined things, hoping to find happiness in intellectual pursuits, friendships, and in pure human loves. These more evolved types get much more pleasure through the senses than do those who are more elemental, but they are capable also of greater and more acute suffering. They can derive great pleasure from a picture gallery, whereas a savage would see nothing interesting at all: they can also suffer from things which a savage would not be capable of feeling. Yet, in spite of this developed refinement and ability to derive pleasure from art, science, literature, etc., happiness is still as far off as ever. All attempts at finding happiness lead finally to "emptiness." There is no satisfaction, either in wealth and all that it can command, getting on in life, or in fame and power. They allure at first and promise happiness, but they fail us, and finally are seen to be but vanity and vexation of spirit.

This desire for happiness is good, for it leads us through innumerable experiences so that the soul can realize, by practical experience, the emptiness of all self-seeking, and thus learn wisdom. After running the whole gamut of experience the soul learns at last that happiness is not something that can be found by seeking it, but is an inward mental state.

Although work, well done, brings a quiet sense of satisfaction, and success in one's career may also be a source of gratification for a short time, yet even these cannot satisfy the deep longing of the soul.

Happiness, however, is to be found in service. Not if we seek happiness in service, and serve in order to be happy, but if we serve others for the sake of serving we find the only happiness that will endure and satisfy.

One has only to observe the lives of those who are always selfishly seeking and grabbing, who are hard in their dealings, and always "looking after number one," in order to see how impossible it is for self-seekers to be happy. It does not matter whether they acquire riches or remain poor—they are equally unhappy. In contrast to this, you have only to go out of your way to do a kind and perfectly disinterested action and experience the glow of sheer happiness that it brings, in order to realize that you are dealing with a law of life that is as sure and unalterable as the law of gravitation.

There must be a purpose in life, and this must have for its object the betterment of the lives of others, either few or many. The law of service must be obeyed, otherwise there can be no happiness. This may fill some readers with dismay, for they may be employed in an occupation that apparently does no good to anybody. They may feel that if they were engaged in some noble enterprise for the uplift of humanity, then they could truly serve, but in their present occupation this is impossible. To think thus is very natural, yet the truth is we can all obey the law of service, and can begin now, in our present occupation, no matter what it may be. We have only to do our daily work, not as a task which must be "got through," in order to bring us a living, or because it is expected of us that we should work, but as an offering of love to life and the world, in order to come into harmony with the great law of service.

Our ideas of values with regard to occupations are altogether erroneous, from the "inner wisdom" point of view. The scrubbing of a doorstep, if faithfully done in a true spirit of service, is of as much value and real importance as the writing of a deathless poem, or dying for one's country. We can never truthfully say that one act of service is of greater value, or is more important than another. All that the higher law looks at is the motive. Therefore, if your motive is right, you can be engaged in the humblest and, apparently, most useless occupation, and yet be happy because you satisfy the law of service.

Another road to happiness is the conquest of the lower nature, the overcoming of weaknesses, the climbing to higher and better things. There is intense happiness in realizing daily that old habits are being overthrown, weak points in the character built up, and an ever-increasing state of liberty and freedom entered into. Thank God, we do not have to remain as we once were, but can progress upwards, indefinitely, for there is no limit to our upward climb.

But there is a state that is far higher than happiness, and this is JOY. Happiness comes through service and overcoming, but joy comes only to one who realizes his oneness with his Divine Source. The reality is ineffable joy. Behind this world of shadows is the real, spiritual world of splendour and delight. When the soul, after its immense journey through matter, time and space, at last finds its way back to its Divine Source, it becomes aware of this intense joy, too great to be described in words. It not only realizes that the reality is joy, and the universe filled, not with groans or sighing, but with the sweet, quiet laughter of freed souls! it also is filled itself with this ineffable joy.

What has all this got to do with practical, everyday life, it may be asked? Everything, for the one who possesses this quiet joy can never be defeated in life's battles. He has something within him that can never be quenched and which will lead him from victory to victory.

# XII.

## THE USE AND MISUSE OF MENTAL AND SPIRITUAL POWERS

The average individual knows nothing of mental forces, and, although he may suffer from the effects of unconscious wrong thinking, yet he is in no danger of making deliberate mis-use of the inner powers. One, however, who has learnt how to use these interior forces must be very careful to use them aright or he will find that the invisible powers of mind and spirit are far more powerful and destructive than dynamite. It is not meant by this that he can blow himself up thereby, but it does mean that he can injure himself, not only in this life, but for ages to come, and, in addition, seriously retard his spiritual evolution.

All use of the mind to coerce other people or to influence them by means of suggestion, not for their benefit, but for your advantage, is highly destructive, not to them actually, but to you. On the face of it, it looks an easy road to success and prosperity, but, actually, it leads to failure and poverty. The mis-use of the mental powers in this way is really a form of black magic, and the fate of all black magicians is very terrible. Even the use of the mind to coerce other people for their good is not desirable. It never does any real good, although it may seem beneficial for a time, and its use, therefore, is to be deprecated. Healing, so-called, by hetero-suggestion, is not permanent, for as soon as the healer ceases to "pump" suggestion into the patient the latter begins to relapse into his former state. Far better results accrue if the patient is taught to use auto or self-suggestion for himself. It is seen, then, that the use of the mind to influence others is distinctly harmful if it is used selfishly, and of no real use if used unselfishly. Hypnotism is harmful, no matter which way it is used, and is also detrimental to the patient. Because of this some of our more thoughtful neurologists have given up its use.

We have no right to endeavour to influence other people by the use of our inner forces, even if our object is their good. Each soul has the right to live its life in its own way, and choose for itself either good or evil. That is the object of life, so that each evolving soul should learn wisdom through the lessons learnt as a result of its own mistakes. Far worse is it if others are coerced, not in order to help them, but to defraud them or to make them buy goods they do not require, or sign agreements they would not otherwise put their name to.

One who misuses his mental and spiritual powers literally smashes his life up. He works against the laws of life and the universe, and encompasses his own ruin.

There is, however, a far more subtle way of misusing the mental and spiritual forces than by coercion, mind domination and hetero-suggestion. This method is equally destructive, and if persisted in builds up a painful future. With this method other people are not influenced or dominated, but the finer forces of Nature are coerced by the human will. Mental demands are made on the invisible substance from which, we are told, all things are made, and wealth is compelled to appear. In addition to this, sickness, so it is claimed, is banished, and the invisible forces of life are compelled to operate in such a way as to make life's pathway a bed of roses, without thorns, so that life becomes shorn of all its discipline and experience.

Its devotees "enter the Silence," and there visualize exactly what they think they want, and compel it to appear, in material form, by the strength of their desire or through the exercise of their will.

Some followers of this cult may be able to make an apparent success of it, but I have never yet met any. If they do, however, they will live to regret it, for they are merely practitioners of black magic. Their efforts are of the same nature as sorcery. All such methods build up a heavy debt of future suffering, and seriously hinder the soul in its evolutionary journey.Entering the Silence is a good thing: it is really entering the inner silence of the soul, the inner sanctuary where the Divine Spirit abides in fulness. To mis-use this inward power for selfish and material ends, and for forcing our human will upon life, so as to make it conform to what we think it ought to be is a crime of the first magnitude, which can result only in ultimate failure and disaster.

# XIII.

## OVERCOMING LIMITATIONS AND AWAKENING INWARD POWERS

Limitations can be overcome through a realization of Truth. When we say this it is taken for granted that every effort will be made on the physical plane. It is necessary to bathe, exercise and breathe fresh air in order to be well: it is equally necessary to work hard, and to give the best of which we are capable, in service, in exchange for that which we receive in the way of supply, if we are to be successful. If you keep a gardener, you must pay him. The money that you pay him is part of what you have earned by the sweat of your brain. Therefore you exchange the work of your brain for the labour of his hands, and you are mutually helped and helpful to one another, both giving and receiving, and each one serving life according to his ability. Taking all this for granted, we will pass on to the metaphysical side of our subject. This, by the way, is vastly the more important, but the outer, practical work is indispensable nevertheless.

In order to overcome limitations it is necessary to know the Truth and to live in the consciousness of It. For instance, if ill-health is our limitation, then, in order to become free it is necessary that we live in the consciousness of the Wholeness of God and His Divine Idea. If our limitation be restricted means, it is necessary that we live in the consciousness of the inexhaustible and unlimited nature of the Substance from which the Creator brings everything into manifestation. If our limitation is disharmony and unhappiness, then we must become attuned to the Divine harmony in such a way and to such an extent as to cause it to be reflected into the outward life. No matter what our limitation may be, we can find liberation and deliverance by looking to our Divine Source, realizing that in the Perfect Reality all our wants are supplied, and then living in the consciousness of this truth.

Ill-health is, apart from physical causes, an outward sign of an inward warfare or disharmony, caused by wrong thoughts, emotions, beliefs and attitude of mind and soul towards life and God. In other words, the life is lived in an "error" consciousness of disease and sickness. First, the inward life has to be adjusted in such a way as to harmonize with the laws of our own being and the Divine purpose of life. There must be an inward surrender to the love principle, after which the thoughts must be brought under control so that health-destroying emotions may no longer impair the health. Further, the whole consciousness must, as often as possible, be raised to a realization of the perfect Wholeness which is the reality. If this course is persevered with, a consciousness of health and wholeness becomes a permanent mental state, with the result that health becomes manifested in the life. The outward life is always a reflection or external manifestation of what we are within, or our state of consciousness. Therefore everything depends upon which kind of consciousness it is in which we live.

One who lives in the mental atmosphere of Divine Wholeness, health and harmony, unconsciously directs all the inner forces of nature into health channels. On the other hand, one who lives in a mental atmosphere of ill-health, as sick and unhealthy people very often do, unconsciously directs all his sub-conscious activities in such a way as to produce sickness and disease.

Again, with regard to lack of means, this state also can be overcome, spiritually, only by living in a higher consciousness of abundance and sufficiency. This affects, unconsciously, every action in such a way as to bring about a better state of affairs. On the other hand, one who lives in a mental atmosphere of limitation and lack, unconsciously directs all his actions towards the production, in his life, of penury and restricted means.

The same rule applies, no matter what the limitations of one's life may be. Freedom can be gained only by realizing the truth about life and being. When we realize the truth, live in the consciousness of it, and become obedient to the laws of life and being, the life becomes increasingly free. This does not mean that if we are plain of feature, and of a stumpy figure, that we shall become beautiful and graceful; but it does mean that these so-called drawbacks will no longer fetter us, and that others will see in us something far better than mere regularity of feature and beauty of form. When the soul is alive and the life filled with love, the homeliest face becomes attractive. Neither does it mean that we shall not suffer bereavements and sorrows, difficulties and adversities, but it does mean that we shall cease intensifying these things and creating further troubles by taking life's discipline in the wrong spirit. It also means that we shall be able to overcome all life's difficulties and trials, become a conqueror in the strife, and, in so doing, build up character. Thus the storms of life, instead of destroying us, can succeed only in making us stronger. Thus our fate depends not on the storms of life, but upon how we meet them.

If we give in to them, or, thinking that they are evil and not a necessary discipline, rebel against them and resist them, then we become shipwrecked on a desolate shore. If, however, we are armed with the knowledge of truth we can set our sails in such a way as to compel the storms of life actually to help us towards the desired haven.

The first step in the direction of knowledge of the truth is right thinking. Every negative thought must be transmuted into its positive opposite,* for instance, hate and dislike into love and goodwill, fear into confident trust, poverty into abundance, evil into absolute good, and so on. This will be found to be not easy, but it is possible, and the power to control one's thoughts increases if one perseveres continually, with the passing of the years. A beginner cannot, naturally, expect to be able to exercise the same control as one who has been perseveringly seeking self-mastery for years, but he can make substantial progress and learn from day to day.

*See also "The Power of Thought" by the same author.

The result of thinking in this way is surprising. The reversal of thought may appear at first to be simplicity itself, and to lead nowhere in particular, but after a time the vastness of the subject becomes almost appalling. The cultivation and practice of right thinking gradually lead to a knowledge of the Truth. Not an intellectual knowledge of truth, but a realization, by the soul, of the Truth. This is the knowing of the Truth which sets men free. We can then look through all the ages and know that all is well. The heavy burden which has oppressed us so long, rolls from our shoulders, and we become free.

## AROUSING INWARD POWERS

Man is heir to wonderful and illimitable powers, but until he becomes aware of them and consciously identifies himself with them, they lie dormant and unexpressed, and might just as well not exist at all as far as their use to man, in his unawakened state, is concerned. When, however, man becomes awakened to the great truth that he is a spiritual being: when he learns that the little petty self and finite personality are not his real self at all, but merely a mask to the real man: when he realizes that the Spiritual Ego, a true Divine Spark of, or branch or twig of the Eternal Logos,* is his real Self: when he understands that his body is not himself, that his mind is not himself, that even his soul is not himself, being but vehicles through which he seeks expression, but that he is spirit, deathless, diseaseless, eternal, forming an integral part of the One Spirit and being identical with It, he enters a new life of almost boundless power.

* "I am the Vine, ye are the branches."—Jesus

It is unwise to engage in any mystical practices in an attempt to "force" development and unfoldment. Mystic trances are highly dangerous and are also unnecessary. Psychic experiences and the awakening of psychic centres are also dangerous and lead away from our goal. Breathing exercises, whose object is to awaken inward powers, are highly dangerous and are to be condemned in consequence.

The cultivation of negative passivity such as inhibiting all thought and making oneself quite passive and open to any influence, is also highly dangerous and should be strictly avoided.

In place of all these unwise practices a short time should be set aside each night and also morning, if possible, for getting into touch with Reality. You should then endeavour to realize that the body, mind and soul are but vehicles of expression, mere servants of the true Self or Ego. This will bring about in time, a consciousness of identity with the One Eternal Spirit. What Jesus called "our Father in Heaven."

One might proceed after this fashion:

"My body is not myself, but is merely something that enables me to live this material life and gain experience.

"My mind is not myself, but merely an instrument which I use and which obeys my will.

"My soul is not myself, but merely a garment of my spirit.

"My will is not myself, but is something of which I, the true Self, make use."

And so on. By this means you gradually approach the great truth which cannot be put into words and which can only become yours through realization or inward spiritual understanding.

In addition one can use a positive statement of Truth, reverently, but with full confidence, such as: "I am a branch in the True Vine."

In course of time you will become possessed of a feeling of tremendous and unlimited power and security. This is a great responsibility for this power must be used only in service and not for selfish purposes. If it is used for the acquisition of wealth and the gaining of temporal power, great disaster will be the inevitable result. Yet, if used aright, it is bound to have a great, though unconscious, influence for good on the life, and for this you are not responsible. Constantly endeavour to serve and bless others, then, because you do not seek them, crowds of blessings will come into your life unbidden, great happiness being one of the chief.

Having found the kingdom of heaven it will be your experience that all needed good will be added unto you.

This power may also be used to strengthen character, to overcome in the conflicts of the soul, and to build up the spiritual body which will be our vehicle of expression in higher realms.

❑❑❑